HERITAGE CRAFTS TODAY

Pressed Flower Art

Pressed Flower Art

Tips, Tools, and Techniques for Learning the Craft

W. EUGENE BURKHART JR.

Photography by Kevin Brett

STACKPOLE
BOOKS

For my parents
Warren E. Burkhart Sr. and Elizabeth I. Burkhart

Copyright © 2008 by Stackpole Books

Published by
STACKPOLE BOOKS
5067 Ritter Road
Mechanicsburg, PA 17055
www.stackpolebooks.com

Printed in China

10 9 8 7 6 5 4 3 2 1

FIRST EDITION

Cover design by Tracy Patterson

Frontispiece: Curry botanical by W. Eugene Burkhart Jr.

Library of Congress Cataloging-in-Publication Data

Burkhart, W. Eugene.
   Pressed flower art : tips, tools, and techniques for learning the craft / W. Eugene Burkhart Jr. ; Photography by Kevin Brett. — 1st ed.
      p. cm. — (Heritage crafts today.)
      ISBN-13: 978-0-8117-0319-2 (hardcover, spiral binding)
      ISBN-10: 0-8117-0319-3 (hardcover, spiral binding)
   1. Pressed flower pictures. 2. Nature craft. I. Title.

SB449.3.P7B87 2008
745.92'8—dc22
                                        2007040210

CONTENTS

ACKNOWLEDGMENTS

I am grateful to Kyle Weaver of Stackpole Books for developing this much-needed series on heritage crafts and selecting me as the author of this pressed flower volume. Thanks to Ray and Pat Oxenford for putting me in touch with him. Also at Stackpole, I appreciate the work of designer Tracy Patterson, art director Caroline Stover, and copyeditor Joyce Bond.

I thank the Temple Greenhouse and the Wolter family for their help in growing plants for my numerous projects and Nature's Pressed Flowers, Inc., for its contribution of pressed plant material.

Thanks also to my parents, Warren E. Burkhart Sr. and the late Elizabeth I. Burkhart, for allowing me to pursue my interests and always being available with love, support, guidance, and help with my endeavors. It is my great honor to dedicate this book to them.

INTRODUCTION

Nature]
a sho
wonderful ;
longer time
flower desi;
cutwork de:
plant, with :

wer designs include natural, conventional, geomet-
:, and abstract forms. In this traditional form of
esign, you use several varieties of flowers. The intri-
te cutwork designs are the modern form of pressing.
sually the artist first draws a scene, still life, or other
sign on paper, and then determines what plant mate-
il is needed. Often pieces of plant material are cut

ssed flower designs in his studio.

Botanical. *This scarlet sage salvia botanical by Burkhart exhibits the entire plant, including the root system.*

Whole flower design. *This lovely design by Burkhart titled* Along the Road, *was made with columbine, basket of gold, and speedwell.*

using scissors to create the exact sizes and shapes needed to complete the design.

People have pressed and preserved plant material for centuries, both for science and for show. One of the oldest pressed plant specimens ever discovered was in an Egyptian tomb, dating to around 300 B.C. Botanists around the world made pressed botanicals for collections of specimens and herbariums as early as 1500 A.D. Others pressed plants to create decorative designs. During the Victorian era it was popular among women to create beautiful whole flower pictures from plant material they had picked on walks and then pressed.

One famous practitioner of the art was Princess Grace of Monaco, who was the first president of the garden club she founded there. In the 1970s, she learned to press flowers from a friend from her native town of Philadelphia. Her wonderful pressed designs were colorful and usually included a blend of textures.

My interest in growing flowers and plants and in various forms of floral design, both two- and three-dimensional, has spanned more than five decades. During my early childhood, my grandmother, the late Leuanna Gerhart, introduced me to gardening, floral design, and pressing. At age six, I entered my first flower show. It

Cutwork design. *Burkhart used cut plant materials to make this picture, titled* Moonlight. *The moon is made from pansy; the trees from fig, maidenhair fern, poinsettia foliage, and polka-dot plant; the arbor from basil; the steps from dusty miller and basil; the pond from delphinium; and the garden flowers from blue salvia, coral bells, and verbena.*

was staged by the Women's Club of Muhlenberg Township in Berks County, Pennsylvania, of which my mother, the late Elizabeth I. Burkhart, was a member. The entry was a fresh flower arrangement in a seashell. I received third prize for my efforts. When I was a teenager, my grandmother encouraged me to experiment with different methods of drying and pressing the beautiful flowers from our gardens. While attending college, I pressed many specimens for plant identification in my horticulture classes.

In the early 1970s, I began competing in the Philadelphia Flower Show with three-dimensional arrangements. I was always amazed by the entries in the pressed flower division and about a decade later, I finally felt that I had mastered the art well enough to submit my first pressed flower entry. It did not win a prize, but I was pleased with my design. I won my first blue ribbon in the pressed flower division a few years later and have continued to win for more than twenty years.

During this time, I was honored to meet pressed flower artist and International Pressed Flower Art Society president Nobuo Sugino from Japan, who invited me to exhibit and lecture at the 1st International Pressed Flower Art Exhibition in Nagano. I was honored to have the chance to share my designs and techniques with the people of Japan, and it was an unforgettable experience. Over the years, I have had many more opportunities to exhibit my designs throughout the United States and the world. I presently work full-time pressing flowers. In 2006, I decided to spend more time teaching the art from my studio at the GoggleWorks Center for the Arts in Reading, Pennsylvania.

In this book I'll teach you how to press and dry various types of plant material so that you can use them to create artistic designs for yourself, your family, and your friends. You'll learn in the following pages my special techniques for creating botanicals, whole flower designs, and intricate cutwork designs.

Tools and Materials

If you don't have your own garden, plants and flowers are available at local garden centers. The tools you need for pressing them are easy to find around your home or at a craft or office-supply store. If you can't find what you need, see the Supplies and Resources section at the back of this book.

FRESH PLANT MATERIAL

When pressing flowers and foliage, it's important to use fresh plant material to obtain good results. Gather the material from your garden or purchase freshly cut plant material from your local florist. For a variety of pressed specimens, see the next chapter on pressing plant material.

Left: *These daffodils are in excellent condition.*

Below: *Daffodils like these are poor specimens and should not be pressed.*

PRESSES

You can purchase flower presses at a craft store or garden center. They are available in different sizes and usually include blotter paper and cardboard. Approximate cost ranges from $10 for a small press to $25 for a large one.

You can use telephone books to press plant material that is thin. They are made from newsprint paper, which will absorb the moisture of the plant material. Do not use books that have glossy paper. Ask your friends to save their old telephone books for your new craft projects.

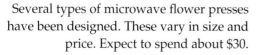

Several types of microwave flower presses have been designed. These vary in size and price. Expect to spend about $30.

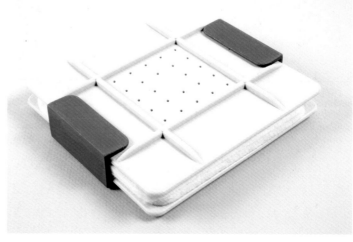

NEWSPRINT PAPER

If you're using a telephone book and not a press, you need a 9 x 12-inch tablet of newsprint paper for pressing plant material. It should be plain if you're pressing white or light-colored flowers. Approximate cost is $1.

TRACING PAPER

Tracing paper is an easy way to reproduce your drawing or part of the design. Approximate cost of a tablet is $4.

DRAWING PAPER

A 9 x 12-inch tablet of 80-pound drawing paper will meet most of your needs. You may use other sizes or weights of paper if you already have some on hand. Approximate cost is $6.

WATERCOLOR PAPER

Use watercolor paper as the surface for your designs, gluing the plant material onto this paper. It is available in several sizes and weights, but I suggest buying a 9 x 12-inch tablet of 140-pound acid-free paper. Approximate cost is $7.

CRAFT PAPER

If you need a colored background for a design, use acid-free craft paper, which is available in different sizes. Approximate cost is $1 for a 12 x 12-inch sheet.

RULER AND TAPE MEASURE

A common ruler and tape measure are sufficient for measuring paper, mats, and picture frames. There is no need to purchase special or more expensive measuring devices. Approximate costs are $1 for a 12-inch ruler and $4 for a tape measure.

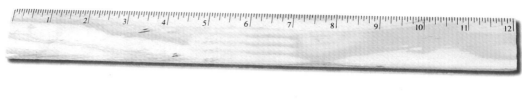

TWEEZERS

Tweezers are helpful to handle the plant material and come in different sizes. Approximate cost ranges from $7 for 4-inch tweezers to $10 for 6-inch tweezers.

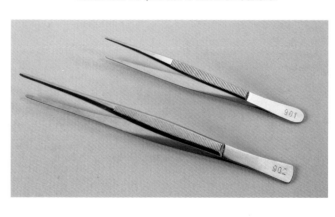

PENCILS AND MARKERS

In most cases, a common number 2 pencil is fine for drawing your designs. If you need a darker image, you can use a marker. A marker might also be helpful when tracing a design. Approximate cost $1.

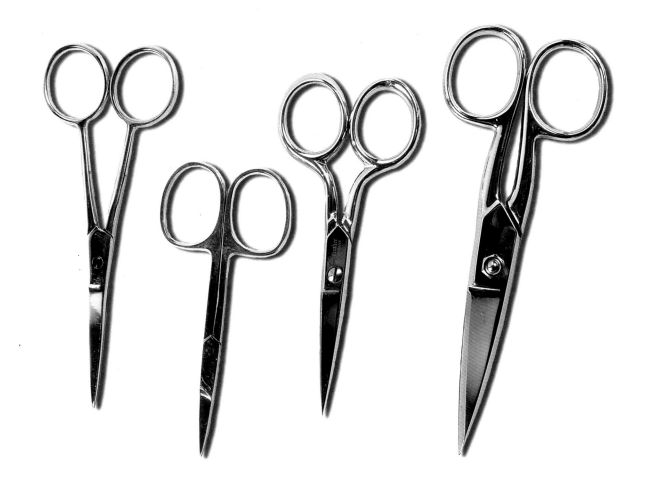

SCISSORS

There are many types and styles of scissors. I've found that Gingher scissors are some of the best to cut the patterns for the intricate cutwork. Approximate cost ranges from $25 for 4-inch Gingher embroidery scissors to $27 for 5-inch. Approximate cost of the less expensive Jo-Ann embroidery scissors is $6 for a 4$^{1}/_{2}$-inch pair.

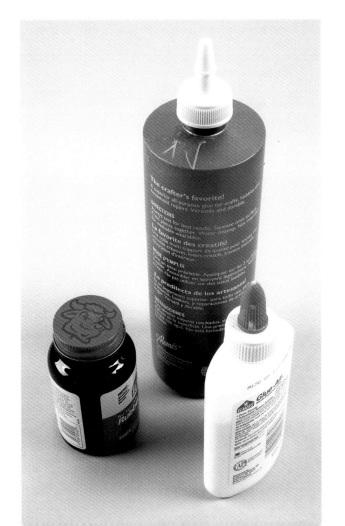

WHITE GLUE, RUBBER CEMENT, AND TACKY GLUE

White glue is the most commonly used adhesive for pressed flower designs. Blue flowers, such as hydrangea, sometimes change color when white glue is used. In these cases, you'll need rubber cement. For plant material that is thick or heavy, use Tacky Glue to keep it in place. Approximate cost of each glue is $1.50 to $1.75.

15

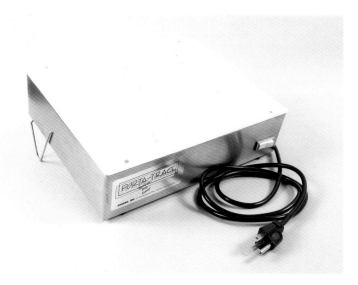

LIGHT BOX
A light box is very helpful when tracing designs. These are available in different sizes. The one pictured here is 9 x 12 inches. Approximate cost is $50.

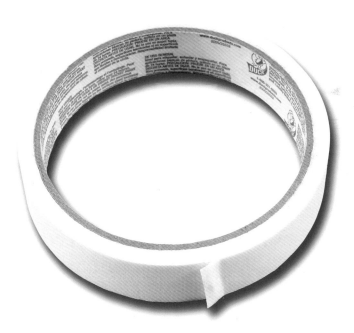

MASKING TAPE
A roll of $^1/_2$-inch masking tape is helpful for most projects, and it's a necessity when using patterns for the intricate cutwork designs. Approximate cost is $1 per roll.

TOOTHPICKS OR LARGE PINS
The pins shown here are $2^1/_2$-inch corsage pins, available at a florist, and toothpicks are the ordinary ones found at a grocery store. You can use either one to apply glue to the plant material. Approximate cost is $1 for a box of toothpicks or $2.50 for a box of corsage pins.

Pressing Plant Material

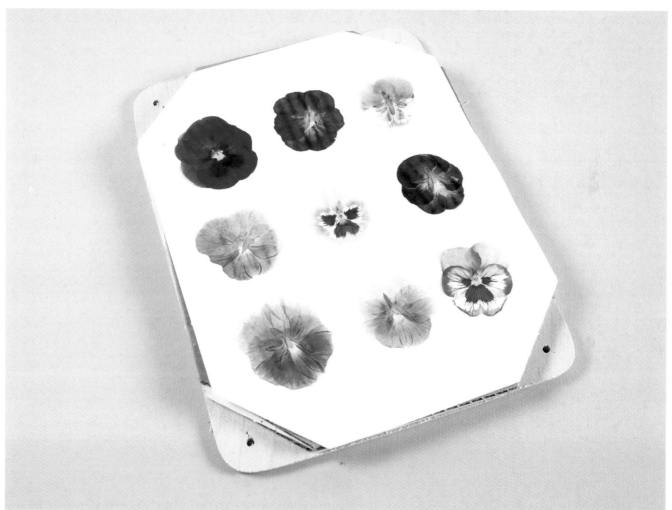

When making pressed flower art, you need to press and dry the plant material before you can create a design. There are three popular methods of pressing: using a flower press, telephone book, or microwave press. A flower press is necessary for whole flowers, whole plants, and plant material that is thick and heavy.

You can use a telephone book for thin plant material or if you are pressing only the petals of flowers for the intricate cutwork. The modern method is the microwave press, of which several types are available. With the microwave press, the plant material dries quickly and better color usually results.

Follow the steps described and illustrated here to successfully dry and press plant material with a flower press.

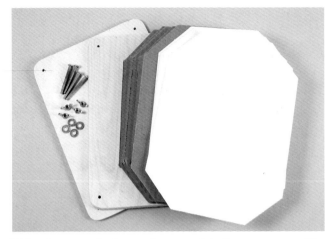

This photograph shows the complete flower press with all the materials.

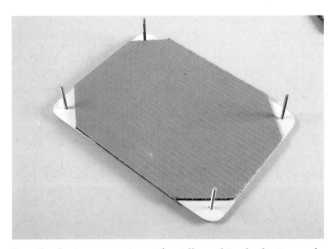

Start by laying one piece of cardboard in the bottom of the press.

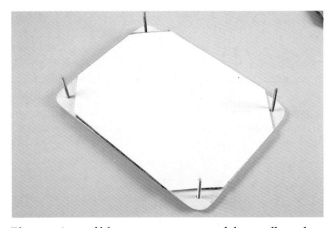

Place a piece of blotter paper on top of the cardboard.

Select fresh and undamaged plant material.

Cut the individual leaves with a scissors. Be sure to keep a small part of the stem on each leaf.

Arrange the fresh flowers and foliage on the blotter paper, placing it facedown.

Press various sizes of plant material in different stages of growth. Leave enough space around the pieces of material so that they don't touch.

Helpful Hints

- Select only the freshest and most nearly perfect plant material. If the plant material is not fresh, the pressed specimens will be of poor quality.
- Pick plant material at midday, after all the dew has evaporated. During this time, the least amount of moisture should be in the plant material.
- A sunny day is best for collecting plant material. Never do this on a rainy day; there will be too much moisture in the plant material.
- Pick plant material of different sizes and in various stages of growth, from buds to open blooms. This will help you create a more interesting design. Open flowers should be at their peak; pick ones that have just opened.

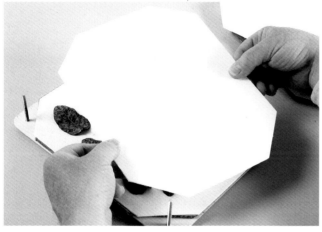

Carefully cover the plant material with a piece of blotter paper by slowly lowering it over the pieces.

Start another layer. In this example, I'm using pansies. Be sure that each piece of plant material is fresh and a good specimen.

Cover the blotter paper with a second piece of cardboard.

Cut the stem off the pansy and set aside. You will press the stems later.

Carefully place the pansy facedown, making sure that it does not touch other plant material.

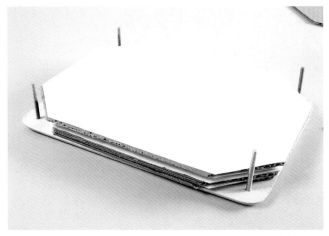

Continue adding more layers of plant material, following the same procedure. This is what that flower press looks like with three layers of plant material, blotter paper, and cardboard.

Follow the same procedure with each pansy, evenly spacing them until you have another layer ready to cover.

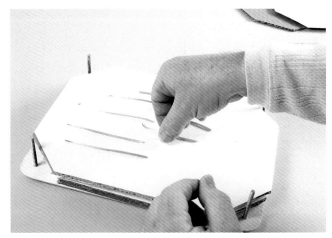

Now arrange the stems on the next piece of blotter paper.

As you did for the first layer, cover the plant material with a piece of blotter paper and then a piece of cardboard.

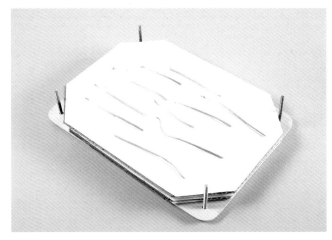

After the stems are arranged as pictured, carefully cover with blotter paper and cardboard.

To press spike flowers, place the first specimen in the middle.

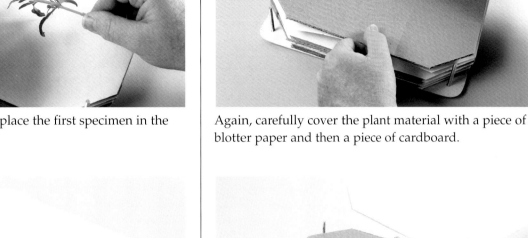

Again, carefully cover the plant material with a piece of blotter paper and then a piece of cardboard.

Then place two other specimens in the opposite direction, spacing them evenly.

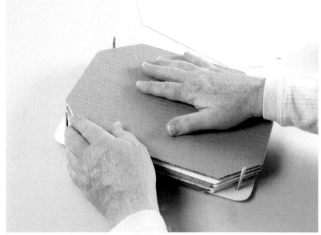

When the press is filled, it is ready to be closed. First, gently press on the top piece of cardboard.

Here is a layer of spike flowers that are properly placed and ready to be covered.

Then place the top of the press on top of the cardboard.

Push the top of the press through the screws.

Here are the pressed spike flowers.

Add the washers and the wing nuts. Tighten the wing nuts on all four corners. Place the press in a dry, warm room. Leave it there for four weeks, tightening the wing nuts daily.

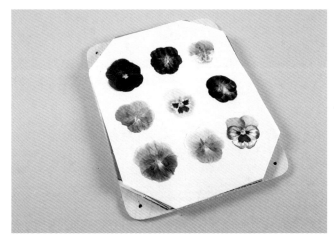

This photo shows the pressed pansies, a few of which have been turned over so that you can see how the face of the flower turns out.

After four weeks, open the press. Here is what the pressed polka-dot leaves look like.

Tips

- After removing the dried pieces of plant material from the press, store them in airtight containers.
- If you put them in folders, be sure the paper is acid-free.
- Keep your pressed plant material out of sunlight.

A telephone book is usually used only for thin pieces of plant material and individual flower petals. If you do not have a flower press, you can press thicker flowers and entire plants in a phone book, but the quality of the dried plant material may vary. Follow these steps to successfully dry and press plant material using a phone book. Be sure all specimens are fresh and in good condition.

When you have completed your first layer of plant material, cover it with a section of about twenty-five more phone book pages.

Start about twenty-five pages from the back of the telephone book.

Now start your next layer. Here I am using hydrangeas, placing the individual flowers facedown on the paper.

Cut the stem off your first flower, here a pansy, and set aside. You will press the stems later on a separate page. Carefully place the flower facedown on the open page of the phone book. Continue with more specimens, making sure that the pieces of plant material don't touch or overlap. Be sure to leave about an inch around the edges of the paper.

Continue creating layers of plant material in this manner. Cover each layer with about twenty-five more pages of the phone book.

For flowers that are light in color, place a facial tissue or a plain piece of newsprint on the page to keep the ink from discoloring them.

A spike flower can also be pressed in a telephone book.

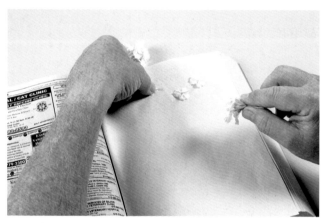

Here the individual white verbena flowers are carefully placed on plain newsprint.

Place the specimens next to the central one in the opposite direction, and cover the plant material with twenty-five pages of the telephone book.

When the page is filled with the white or light-colored flowers, cover them with another facial tissue or piece of newsprint, then with another twenty-five phone book pages.

Here I am pressing a small snapdragon. First check for any broken leaves or damaged blossoms.

With a flower that is full with blossoms, like the snap-dragon, remove some of the individual flowers before pressing.

Write the date and types of plant material on the front of the phone book.

Place the single stalk of flowers on the page and carefully cover with twenty-five pages of the phone book.

Stack several filled telephone books on top of each other in a warm, dry room, and then place at least 15 pounds of weight on the top of the books. Do not open the telephone books for four weeks.

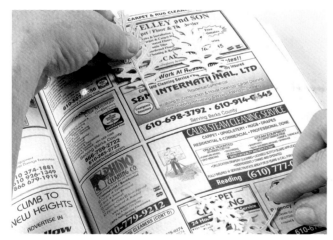

Here some dusty miller leaves are carefully placed face-down on the paper.

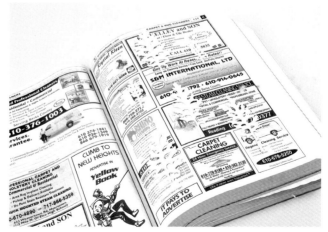

Here is the dusty miller foliage after four weeks of pressing in a telephone book.

Telephone Book Method *continued*

This photo shows the dried, pressed white verbena flowers.

Here are the hydrangea flowers.

Tips

- After removing the plant material from the telephone books, store the plant material in airtight containers.
- Keep out of sunlight.
- When using folders, make sure the paper folders are acid-free.

Microwave Flower Press Method

Several different types of microwave flower presses have been designed. The advantages of using a microwave press are that you get quick results and the color is usually better. Follow the directions included with your microwave press as well as the general instructions for your microwave.

Generally, you start with short bursts at a medium setting, perhaps thirty to sixty seconds. You need to experiment with the timing. Allow the plant material to cool between bursts. Open the press to allow the steam to escape, then repeat the procedure until the plant material is dry, being careful not to burn it. Store the resulting dried plant material in a dry, cool room.

PRESSED FLOWER AND FOLIAGE SPECIMENS

After the flowers and foliage are pressed, they lose their three-dimensional form. Following is a collection of photographs of dried, pressed flowers and foliage to give you an idea of what they will look like and help you decide what types of flowers and plants to grow and collect. In most cases, the common names are given.

Pressed Flowers

Specimens shown actual size

Ageratum

Angelina

Alyssum

Apache plume

Avens

Basket of gold

Baby's breath

Bees plant

Bachelor's button

Bleeding heart

Borage

Boronia

Bells of Ireland

Black-eyed Susan

Bottlebrush

Bougainvillea

Bridal wreath

Buttercup

Calendula

Calla lily

Caspia

Celosia

Cigar flower

Cinquefoil

Columbine

Coral bells

Coreopsis

Daisy

Cosmos

Delphinium

Cyclamen (petals)

Dendrobium

Desert marigold

English Daisy

Dianthus

Fantasia

Dogwood

Forget-me-not

Forsythia

Freesia

Four-o'clock

Fritillaria

Foxglove

Fuchsia

Heather

Gilia

Hibiscus (petals)

Golden chain tree

Hydrangea

Johnny-jump-up

Indian paintbrush

Larkspur

Indian strawberry

Larkspur stalks

Lavender

Lobelia

Leopard lily

Marigold

Mexican heather

Lisianthus

Miniature rose

Nasturtium

Nicotiana

Petunia

Phalaenopsis

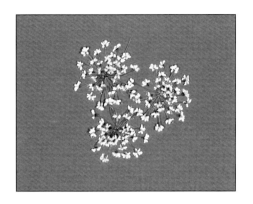

Queen Anne's lace

Phlox

Poinsettia

Primrose

Salvia

Shooting star

Snakeweed

Silver lace vine

Snapdragon

Smoke tree blossoms

Tamarack

Speedwell

Texas bluebonnet

Sunflower

Torenia

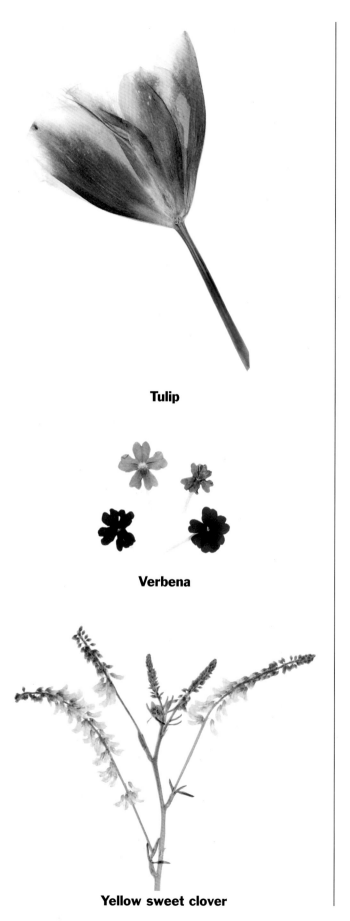

Tulip

Verbena

Yellow sweet clover

Zinnia

Amur maple

Aspen

Artemisia

Baby's tears

Asparagus fern

Basil

Birch

Boston creeper

Bleeding heart

Broom grass

Blood leaf

Buffalo grass

Button fern

Curry

Carolina

Dusty miller

Cedar

Chinese elm

Feather fern

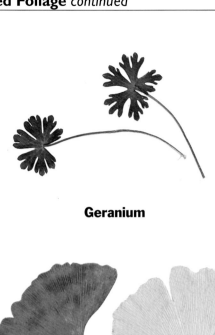

Geranium

Ivy

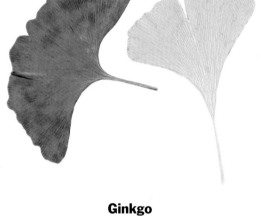

Ginkgo

Hare's tail grass

Hawthorn

Japanese maple

Lamb's ears

Maidenhair fern

Leatherleaf fern

Maple

Licorice

Marjoram

Mimosa

Nerve plant

Mountain fern

Oak

Nasturtium

Oregano

Ornamental pear

Rabbit's foot fern

Parsley

Rain tree

Pine needles

Rombus fern

Rose

Smoke tree

Rosemary

Rue

Stinkgrass

Sumac

Silver leaf

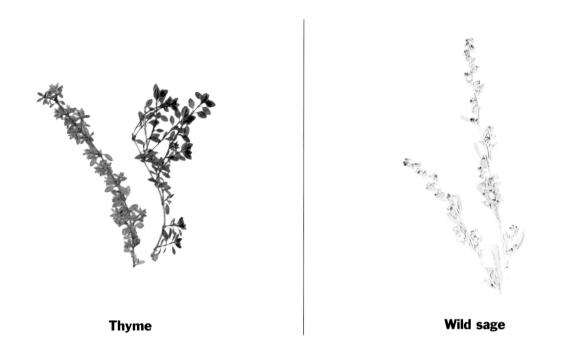

Thyme   **Wild sage**

Tulip

Other Plants and Flowers

Here are some additional plants and flowers that can be used in pressed flower art.

Acacia	Cornflower	Liatris	Rudbeckia
African violet	Creeping zinnia	Lilac	Russian sage
Alstroemeria	Crocus	Lily	Sanvitalia
Aluminum plant	Cypress	Lily of the valley	Sassafras
Anemone	Daffodil	Love-in-a-mist	Scaevola
Anita ivy	Dahlia	Milkweed	Scotch broom
Apple	Dracaena	Ming aralia	Sea lavender
Ash	Daylily	Mock orange	Shasta daisy
Aster	English ivy	Monkey flower	Shrimp plant
Astilbe	Euonymus	Morning glory	Snakeroot
Azalea	False aralia	Mountain ash	Snowdrop
Balloon flower	False heather	Mullein	Snow-on-the-
Balsam	Feverfew	Narcissus	mountain
Bee balm	Firecracker plant	Needlepoint ivy	Solidago
Beech	Flame violet	Nigella	Spider flower
Bell flower	Flax	Norfolk Island pine	Spirea
Bird of paradise	Flowering maple	Ornamental sage	Star-of-Bethlehem
Blackberry lily	Gaillardia	Oriental poppy	Statice
Blanket flower	Geum	Ostrich fern	Stephanotis
Boston ivy	Gerbera daisy	Oxalis	Stock
Boxwood	Gladiolus	Palm	Strawberry
Bugleweed	Globe amaranth	Parlor palm	Sweet gum
Burning bush	Glory flower	Passionflower	Sweet pea
Butterfly bush	Goat's beard	Peony	Sweet William
California poppy	Goldenrod	Periwinkle	Tansy
Candle plant	Grape hyacinth	Piggyback plant	Thunbergia
Candytuft	Grape ivy	Pilea	Trumpet vine
Canterbury bells	Grasses	Plantain lily	Variegated table fern
Carnation	Gypsophila	Polka-dot plant	Veronica
Carrot foliage	Heliotrope	Poplar	Viola
Cherry	Hollyhock	Poppy	Violet
Chicory	Honesty	Portulaca	Weeping fig
Chinese lantern	Honeysuckle	Potentilla	Weigela
Christmas rose	Iceland Poppy	Purple velvet plant	Willow
Chrysanthemum	Iris	Ranunculus	Wisteria
Cineraria	Lady's mantle	Rhododendron	Yarrow
Clematis	Lamium	Rosary vine	Yellow ripple ivy
Clover	Lantana	Rose of Sharon	
Clubmoss	Lenten rose	Rubrum lily	

Making Pressed Botanicals

The botanical is the oldest form of pressing. A botanical shows the parts of the plant and its flowers and may also include the root system. Botanists have been creating pressed botanicals for centuries for collections of specimens and for herbariums. Botanicals have come to be appreciated as an art form as well and will make a nice addition to your home or office decor.

Following are step-by-step instructions for creating a pressed botanical. The text and photographs demonstrate how to prepare the plant for pressing, how to press it using either a flower press or telephone book, and how to prepare the pressed plant for framing. For the best results, use a flower press. For either method, you need a good specimen of a plant growing in your garden or a pot.

Above: *A botanical of a miniature rose.*

To demonstrate how to make botanicals with a flower press, I'm starting with a curry plant growing in a container.

Take the plant out of the container. Begin gently removing some of the soil, then place the roots in water to soak for a few minutes. Wash off the remaining soil with running water. Try to remove every particle of soil around the root system.

Place two pieces of blotter paper and a piece of cardboard in the press.

Arrange the plant on the blotter paper. If the plant is too large, you can cut some of the material into separate pieces. You can add the extra pieces on the blotter paper, if there is room.

Cover the plant with two more pieces of blotter paper

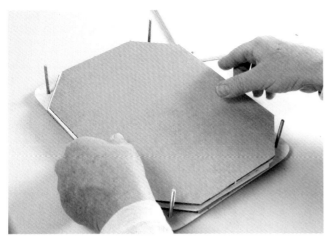

Place another piece of cardboard on top of the blotter paper.

The flower press allows you to press several plants at the same time in layers. Start the next layer by placing two pieces of blotter paper for the second plant.

Clean off the roots of the next plant, and place it on the blotter paper. I'm demonstrating with a torenia. Extra pieces also can be pressed on the same paper.

Cover the plant with two pieces of blotter paper.

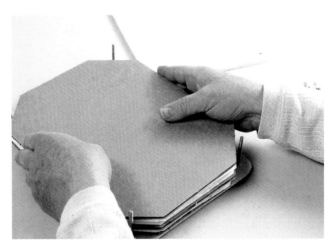

Place a piece of cardboard on top of the blotter paper.

Add two more pieces of blotter paper, then arrange the next plant, a lobelia in this case, on the paper. Cover with two more pieces of blotter paper and another piece of cardboard.

Begin another layer with two pieces of blotter paper, and place the next plant, dusty miller here, on top.

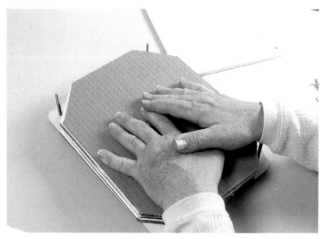

As before, cover with two pieces of blotter paper and cardboard. Then add the top piece of the press and tighten the screws. Place in a dry, warm room for four weeks and tighten the screws daily.

After four weeks, open the press. Here's the pressed botanical curry.

This photograph shows the pressed botanical torenia.

The pressed botanical lobelia looks like this.

And here's the pressed botanical dusty miller.

Gently check each botanical for broken leaves.

Choose a frame that is the correct size for the plant. You may want to mat the plant first. The photograph shows a white mat on top of the watercolor paper serving as a guide for placement. Replace it with a color mat when the botanical is ready to be framed.

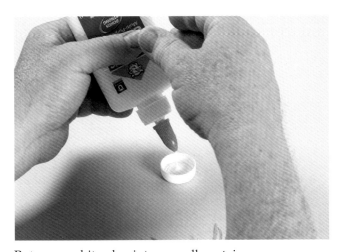

Put some white glue into a small container.

Using a toothpick or pin, place dots of glue on the underside of the leaves.

Also place dots of glue on the root system.

Continue until all the foliage and roots have dots of glue. (If the plant has flowers, put glue on them, too.)

Place the botanical on the watercolor paper.

You may need to apply additional glue.

Hold the foliage in place for a minute or two, especially necessary if the plant material is thick or heavy.

Here's the completed curry botanical in a frame with color mat.

I'll demonstrate how to make a botanical using a telephone book with a cigar flower plant growing in a container.

Take the plant out of the container. Begin gently removing some of the soil, then place the roots in water to soak for a few minutes.

Wash off the remaining soil with running water. Try to remove every particle of soil around the root system.

If the plant is too large for the phone book, trim off some pieces. You will also press them in the book separately.

After the roots are dry, the plant is ready for pressing. Start about fifty pages in from the back of the book. If needed, cut and arrange the root system in the book.

Use about fifty pages of the phone book to cover the plant. Place any pieces of the plant you trimmed off in separate layers about fifty pages apart. When all the plant material is in the book, put it in a warm, dry room, and place at least 15 pounds of weight on top of the book. For flowers that are light in color, place a plain piece of newsprint on the page to keep the ink from discoloring them.

After four weeks, open the phone book.

Gently examine the plant for any broken flowers or foliage.

Choose a frame that is the correct size for the plant. You may want to mat the plant first. The photograph shows a white mat on top of the watercolor paper serving as a guide for placement. Replace it with a color mat when the botanical is ready to be framed.

Arrange all the individual pieces of the plant that were cut on the paper before gluing.

Make sure that most of the leaves are facing the correct way.

Starting with the main piece of your specimen, use a toothpick or pin to place dots of glue on the underside of the leaves and flowers.

Follow the same steps to glue and add each piece to the plant.

Also place dots of glue on the root system, if it is still attached.

Place the main piece of your specimen inside the mat area on the watercolor paper.

Here's the completed cigar flower botanical in the frame with a color mat.

Phlox

Dianthus

Verbena

Petunia

Cosmos

Zinnia

Coral bells

Nicotiana

Dusty miller

English ivy

Buttercup

Ageratum

Mexican heather

Rosemary

Polka-dot plant

Lobelia

Nasturtium

Fuchsia

Torenia

Marigold

Celosia

Blue salvia

Snapdragon

Framing

When choosing a frame for a botanical or other pressed flower design, make sure it is the correct size and shape. The frame on the left is too large for this botanical. To correct this problem, I cut the paper to a smaller size and chose a smaller frame for the zinnia botanical.

Making Whole Flower Designs

Since the Victorian era, artists have been creating two-dimensional designs with pressed, dried whole flowers and foliage. The designs may be of natural, conventional, geometric, or abstract form and are typically framed under glass. In this chapter, I will first take you step by step through two projects, and then follow with a variety of designs that you can try on your own, using the plant material you have pressed and the techniques presented in the earlier chapters.

Above: This natural-looking whole flower design has salvia, alyssum, shooting star, coral bells, silver lace vine, rabbit's foot fern, larkspur foliage, maidenhair fern, and licorice.

The Garden is a horizontal pressed flower design. When creating a whole flower design, you start with the placement of the large flowers, and gradually fill in the design with foliage and smaller flowers. By following the steps and referring to the photographs, you will be able to create a beautiful garden scene like this one.

Helpful Hints

- Do not use flowers that are all the same size.
- Do not use flowers that are too small or too large in relation to the overall size of the design.
- Keep the design simple.
- Do not use too many different forms of flowers and foliage.
- Make sure the frame you choose complements the design.

Plant List

Alyssum flowers
Artillery flowers
Blue larkspur
Columbine
Larkspur foliage
Pink larkspur
Rabbit's foot fern

First cut a sheet of watercolor paper to the desired size. The paper I used for this design measures 8 x 20 inches. Begin by arranging pressed, dried blue larkspur flowers on the paper. Then use a toothpick or pin to apply glue to each piece of plant material in turn.

Add columbine flowers to the design, and glue them onto the paper.

Place pink larkspur strategically, then glue to the paper.

Add artillery flowers and glue them in place.

Next, arrange and glue rabbit's foot fern and larkspur foliage.

Finish with alyssum flowers.

Floral Splendor I is a vertical design. After selecting the plant material for the design, start by placing the large flowers, and then add the other flowers and foliage. By following the steps outlined below, you will be able to create a beautiful design similar to the one shown here. Rather than add and glue each flower one by one, as described below, you might find it easier to arrange all the plant material on the watercolor paper first, and then when you are pleased with the design, glue all the pieces onto the paper.

Plant List

Blue larkspur
Blue salvia
Columbine
Coral bells
Larkspur foliage
Pink larkspur

First cut a sheet of watercolor paper to the desired size. The paper I used for this design measures 8 x 20 inches. Begin by arranging pressed, dried blue larkspur flowers on the paper. Then use a toothpick or pin to apply dots of glue to the larkspur, and glue each piece to the paper.

Add columbine flowers to the design, and glue them to the paper.

Place a sprig of pink larkspur, and glue it in place.

Arrange and glue several pieces of blue salvia to the paper.

Finally, add coral bells and larkspur foliage, and glue them to the paper.

By looking at floral design books and magazines, you can find endless ideas for pressed flower designs. At first, it may be easier for you to copy a design or two. To help give you some inspiration, here's a gallery of designs that I have created for you with plant material available from the spring to fall seasons.

Floral Splendor II. *This design is similar to Floral Splendor I, with blue and pink larkspur, coral bells, columbine, and larkspur foliage.*

Summer I. *Here's a design incorporating a variety of summer plants: coreopsis, larkspur, yellow sweet clover, pansy, verbena, coral bells, artillery, salvia, alyssum, rabbit's foot fern, torenia, and maidenhair fern.*

Summer II. *This summery design includes hydrangea, forget-me-not, salvia, coreopsis, pansy, coral bells, alyssum, verbena, and maidenhair fern. The summer designs can be displayed on a wall individually or in a grouping.*

Grandmom's Garden. *This design has three cheery sunflowers surrounded by lupine, salvia, yellow sweet clover, larkspur, columbine, coral bells, miniature rose, and rabbit's foot fern.*

Sunflowers. *This design made solely of sunflowers will brighten up any day.*

Floral Mat I. *You can create decorated mats with pressed plant material for your favorite photographs. This is a right-angle design of dianthus, salvia, larkspur, baby's breath, and maidenhair fern.*

Floral Mat II. *This decorated mat is a garden design with yellow sweet clover, alyssum, verbena, coral bells, bridal wreath, baby's breath, forget-me-not, and maidenhair fern.*

Floral Quilt. *Here's a patchwork quiltlike design using cosmos, pansy, primrose, miniature rose, boronia, scaevola, verbena, mimosa, maple leaves, and maidenhair fern.*

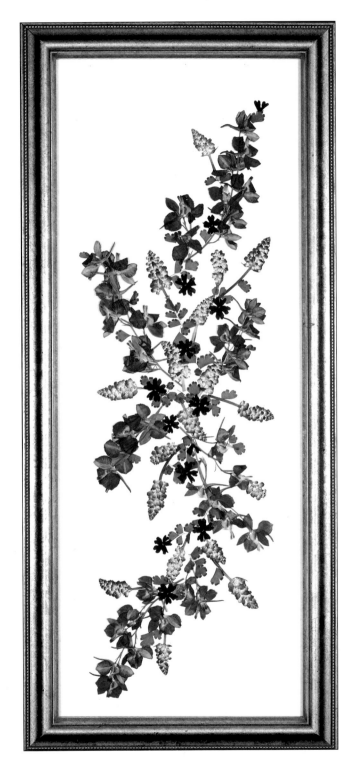

Shades of Blue. *You can create interesting designs using different hues of one color. This design combines various shades of blue, with larkspur, salvia, verbena, and maidenhair fern.*

In the Garden. *This design features fuchsia, basket of gold, torenia, angelina, speedwell, cosmos, and dianthus.*

Autumn Delight. *You can create a design using fall leaves of various colors, in this case Japanese maple, maple, birch, and Chinese elm.*

Fall Beauty. *Here's another fall leaf design, this time with birch, licorice, maple, Chinese elm, and Japanese maple.*

Summer Bouquet. *Make a bouquetlike design, like this one with hydrangea, pansy, primrose, fern, verbena, and dusty miller.*

Small Designs for Cards. *You can create small designs likes these to make your own greeting cards.*
These smaller designs feature buttercups, yellow sweet clover, salvia, verbena, heather, caspia, cosmos, maidenhair fern, pansy, baby's breath, and foxglove.

Large Designs for Cards. *These larger designs intended for cards include heather, alyssum, forget-me-not, salvia, maidenhair fern, verbena, bachelor's buttons, artemisia, and button fern.*

Blue and Gold. *A two-color combination can be striking. This blue and gold design uses cosmos, salvia, rabbit's foot fern, and forget-me-not.*

Simply Beautiful. *Here's another design with a simple color combination, using speedwell, larkspur, four-o'clock, rabbit's foot fern, and alyssum.*

Pansies. *Another idea is to show a flower arrangement in a container, as done here. This design has poinsettia foliage, pansy, forget-me-not, speedwell, pansy foliage, salvia, and maidenhair fern.*

Daylily. *This oriental-looking design is made with tulip foliage, yellow sweet clover, bleeding heart foliage, and daylily.*

Simply Elegant. *Here's a simple but exquisite design featuring zinnia, bleeding heart, coral bells, and bleeding heart foliage.*

Making Cutwork Designs

Cutwork designs are the modern form of pressed flower art, using plant materials to create pictures of all sorts, such as scenes, still lifes, or emblems. The designs can be real or imaginary. You begin by lightly drawing the design on a piece of watercolor paper.

Then make several photocopies of your design to use as patterns. You will glue the dried plant materials to some of the copies and use others to aid you in cutting out the various elements of the design.

Above: This sampler design is made with plant material in the nine blocks: cosmos, pansy, cyclamen, heather, delphinium, rose, marigold, poinsettia, tulip foliage, nasturtium foliage, astilbe foliage, hydrangea, gerbera daisy, and basil. The background of each block is hibiscus.

This project is given in its entirety to demonstrate the cutwork design procedure. You can follow these steps to create any design you wish.

Trace and transfer the drawing of the Pennsylvania Dutch Design onto an 8-inch square of watercolor paper. Also make seven photocopies of the design.

Here's the plant material for this project.

Plant List

Leaves:	Rue, primrose, orange cosmos
Bird's wing:	Orange cosmos
Bird's body:	Yellow cosmos
Bird's tail:	Yellow and orange cosmos
Feet and eye:	Rose
Tulips:	Orange and yellow cosmos, carnation
Teardrop design:	Orange cosmos
Flower:	Golden chain tree
Stems:	Primrose foliage

Use a corsage pin or toothpick to apply the glue to the plant material.

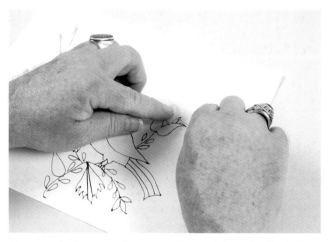

On one photocopy, glue carnation petals onto the tulip design.

Here's the first photocopy with the carnation petals.

On the second copy, glue orange cosmos petals over the tulip design and inside the tail of the bird.

On the third copy, glue orange cosmos petals inside the bird's wing and the teardrop design. Cut a piece of the primrose foliage for the leaf design and glue it on the paper.

On the fourth copy, glue yellow cosmos petals inside the body of the bird. Also glue on orange cosmos petals for the center of the leaf design.

On the fifth copy, glue yellow cosmos petals onto the center of the tail.

On the third copy, tape on patterns of the wing, teardrop, and leaf.

Use the sixth and seventh copies for cutting the various elements to use for patterns. These patterns will aid you in cutting out the pieces with the glued-on plant material. On the first copy, tape a cutout pattern of the tulips over the plant material.

On the fourth copy, tape on patterns of the body of the bird and the center of the leaf design.

On the second copy, tape cutout patterns of the tulips and the tail over the glued-on plant material.

On the fifth copy, tape on a pattern of the center of the tail.

Similarly, cut freehand the pieces needed for the eye and the feet from rose petals.

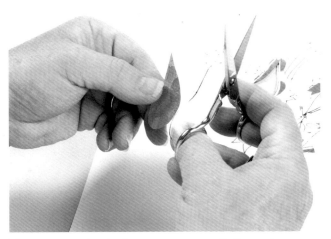

Then use a pair of scissors to cut out all the patterns.

Now you will start gluing all your cutout pieces onto the watercolor paper. First glue the wing onto the body of the bird.

Also use the scissors to cut freehand the stems needed for the design from primrose foliage.

When the glue is dry, apply glue to the body of the bird.

Place the bird in the middle of the watercolor paper.

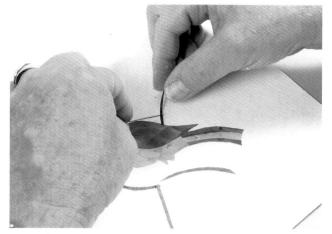

Next glue the stems onto the watercolor paper.

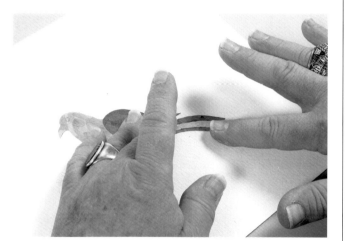

Then glue on the bird's tail.

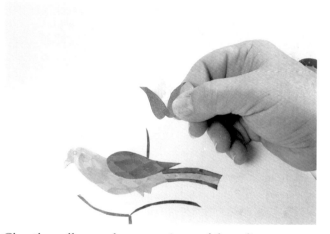

Glue the yellow and orange pieces of the tulips together.

Here's what the design looks like so far.

When the glue is dry, glue the completed tulips onto the watercolor paper.

Glue on the teardrop and the leaf design.

Glue on the small pieces of rose petal to create the feet.

Here's what the design looks like at this stage.

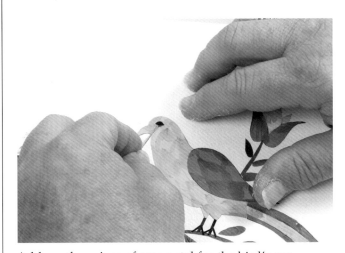

Add another piece of rose petal for the bird's eye.

Glue on the pieces of rue for leaves and add a few golden chain tree flowers.

Here's how the completed design will look.

This project differs in that the garden area and sky are done by gluing all of your plant material directly onto the transferred design on the watercolor paper, rather than using patterns.

The plant material used for this section of the garden is blue salvia, alyssum, maidenhair fern, verbena, and baby's breath.

Plant List

Sky:	Delphinium, hydrangea
Trees:	Maidenhair fern, fern, larkspur foliage, polka-dot plant, nerve plant, verbena foliage
Tree trunks:	Basil, pear leaves
Garden plants and flowers:	
	Nasturtium foliage, Queen Anne's lace, blue salvia, verbena, baby's breath, dianthus, maidenhair fern, alyssum
Animals:	Cyclamen, poinsettia, marigold, verbena

Trace the garden design and copy on watercolor paper, enlarging or reducing as necessary.

Here's a drawing of a portion of the garden to demonstrate this procedure.

Using a toothpick or a pin, apply the glue to the plant material and carefully place on the paper.

Carefully place the plant material on the paper.

Apply the glue to a piece of the maidenhair fern.

Apply the glue to the alyssum flowers.

Apply the glue to a single verbena flower.

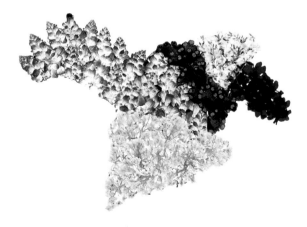

Here's how the completed garden area will look. Follow the same procedure for the sky.

In the next few pages, I provide plant lists and drawings for making a variety of cutwork designs.

Plant List

Clouds:	Pansy
Birds:	Basil
Hat:	Basil, cosmos, fern
Jacket:	Hibiscus, cosmos, delphinium
Face:	Rose
Pants:	Delphinium
Gloves and feet:	Rose
Cornstalks:	Dianthus foliage, grass
Pumpkin:	Cosmos
Wood:	Magnolia
Vegetable foliage:	Maidenhair fern, fern
Vegetables:	Cosmos, verbena

Plant List

Container:	Hydrangea
Oval design:	Rose
Inside oval:	Mixed flowers of bridal wreath, viola, forget-me-not, verbena, larkspur foliage
Plant:	Pansy flowers in various stages of growth, from bud to full bloom, with pansy foliage

Plant List

Background:	Carnation
Heart:	Poinsettia
Tulip:	Poinsettia, rose
Tulip foliage:	Poinsettia foliage
Distelfink:	Alstroemeria, delphinium, hydrangea
Legs and feet of bird:	Basil
Other foliage:	Poinsettia foliage

Plant List

Trees:	Boxwood, parsley, Mexican heather, artemisia
Gazebo:	Tulip foliage
Trellis:	Tulip foliage
Garden sections:	Bachelor button, yellow sweet clover, bridal wreath, verbena, maidenhair fern, heather, alyssum
Wood:	Maple leaves, rose

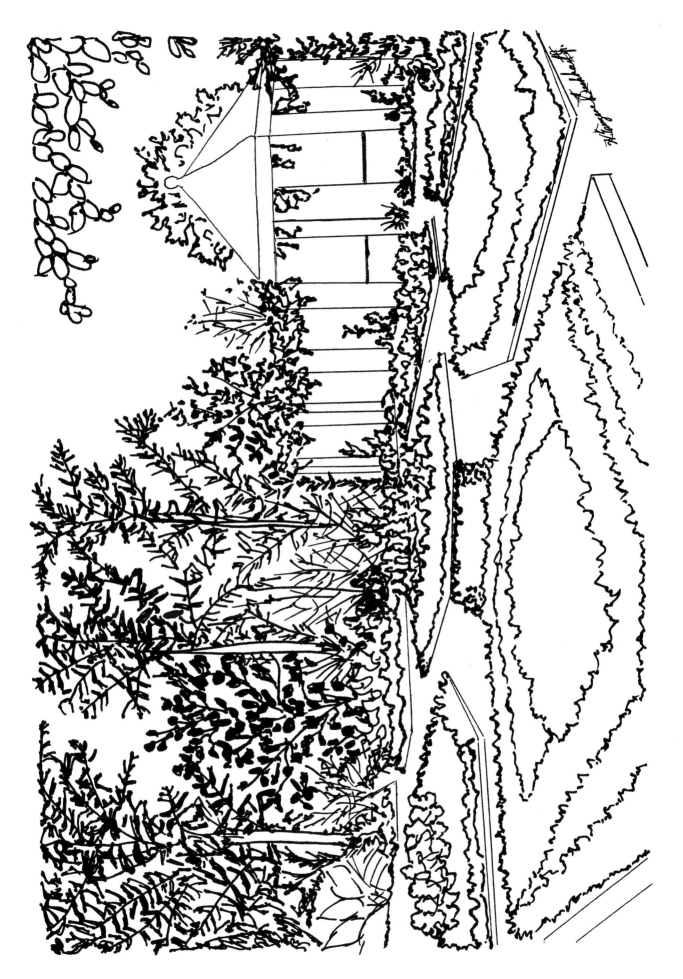

Plant List

Sky:	Pansy
Mountains:	Various varieties of poinsettia
Fields:	Yellow alyssum, fritillaria
Covered bridge:	Poinsettia, basil, cyclamen
Barns:	Poinsettia, cyclamen
Silo:	Cyclamen
Pasture:	Maple leaves, maidenhair fern
Fence:	Rose
Road:	Pear leaves
Flowering trees:	Maidenhair fern, alyssum
Green trees:	Maidenhair fern, parsley
Creek:	Hydrangea

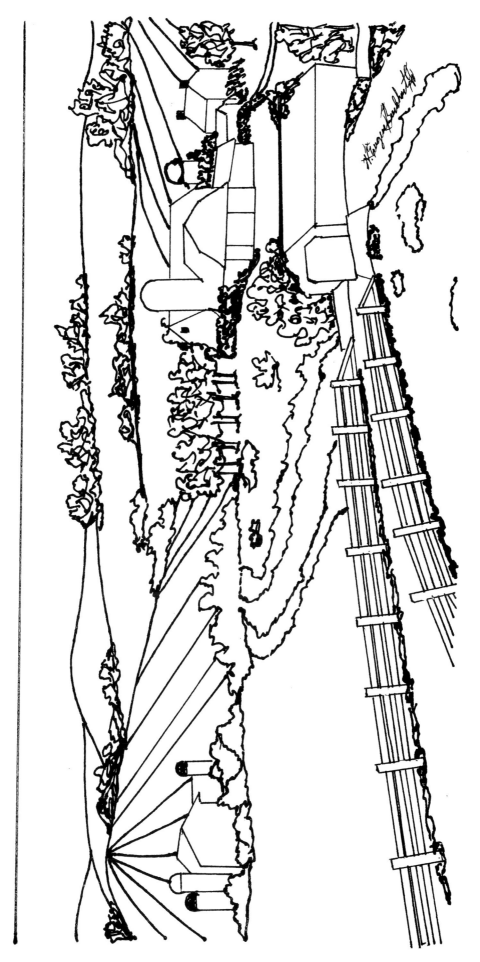

Plant List

Sky:	Pansy, delphinium, hydrangea	Door:	Poinsettia
Trees:	Fern, fig, lamium, maidenhair fern	Walls of cottage:	Carnation
		Stone wall:	Various varieties of poinsettia
Tree trunks:	Basil, tulip foliage	Flowering vines on cottage:	
Flowering trees:	Alyssum, tulip foliage ·		Maidenhair fern, alyssum
Cottage roof:	Fritillaria	Pathway:	Nasturtium foliage
Windows:	Poinsettia	Gardens:	Dianthus, alyssum, salvia, Queen Anne's lace, nerve plant, verbena
Trim around windows:	Basil		

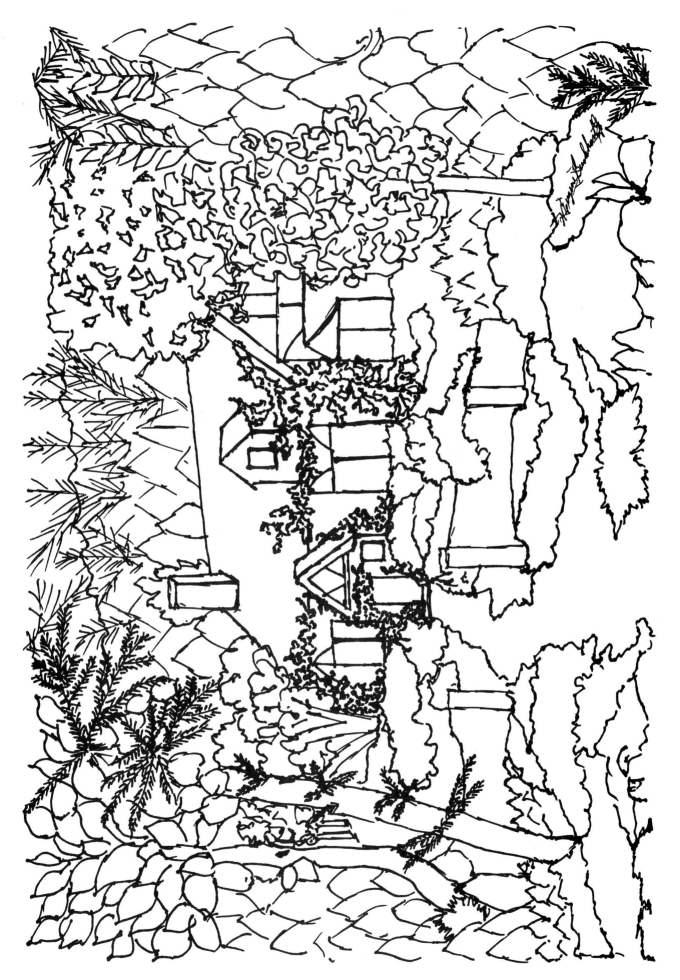

Plant List

Elephant:	Poinsettia
Tiger:	Cosmos
Giraffe:	Cosmos
Monkey:	Rose
Trees:	Maidenhair fern
Tree trunk:	Poinsettia
Plants:	Miniature palm, verbena foliage, larkspur foliage, nerve plant, fern, bottle brush, alstroemeria, primrose, croton, polka-dot plant, mimosa, maple leaves, baby's tears

Plant List

Clouds:	Pansy
Palm trees:	Tulip foliage, palm
Ocean:	Several varieties of delphinium, hydrangea, cyclamen
Rock formations:	Poinsettia
Banana tree:	Poinsettia foliage
Bananas:	Marigold
Garden:	Coral bells, fern, daisy foliage, polka-dot plant, forget-me-not, poinsettia foliage, daisy foliage, alyssum

Plant List

Castle:	Gerbera daisy, hydrangea, basil
Pathway to castle:	Gerbera daisy, basil
Seahorse:	Rose
Seahorse's eye:	Delphinium
Turtle:	Nasturtium foliage, poinsettia foliage, tulip foliage
Fish:	Cosmos, delphinium, larkspur, marigold, cyclamen, gerbera daisy
Treasure chest:	Poinsettia, marigold
Seashells:	Gerbera daisy
Plants:	Nerve plant, ferns, club moss, bear grass, dianthus foliage, parsley

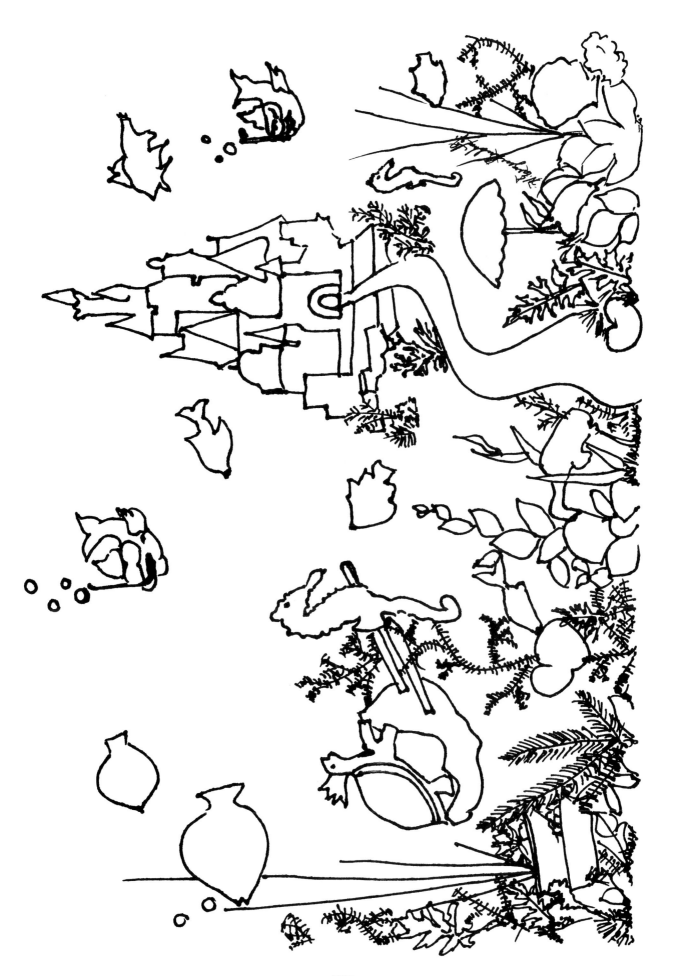

Plant List

Background: Rose
Flowers: Delphinium, rose, heather, silver lace vine, cosmos, cyclamen,
                     poinsettia, bridal wreath
Foliage: Poinsettia, china doll

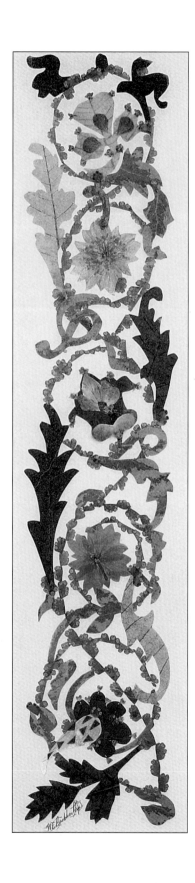

Plant List

Foliage: Maidenhair fern,
        poinsettia, nasturtium
Flowers: Cosmos, poinsettia,
        heather, delphinium,
        basil, pansy

Plant List

Tree:	Baby's tears, maple leaves
Palm tree:	Mimosa
Ocean:	Delphinium, cyclamen
Garden:	Coral bell, blue salvia, verbena, alyssum, rose, Queen Anne's lace, parsley, maidenhair fern
Sand:	Carnation
Diamond Head:	Poinsettia
Clouds:	Pansy

143

Plant List

Ribbon design:	Heather
Clowns:	Cosmos, delphinium, marigold
Fish:	Poinsettia, alyssum
Letter L:	Blood leaf

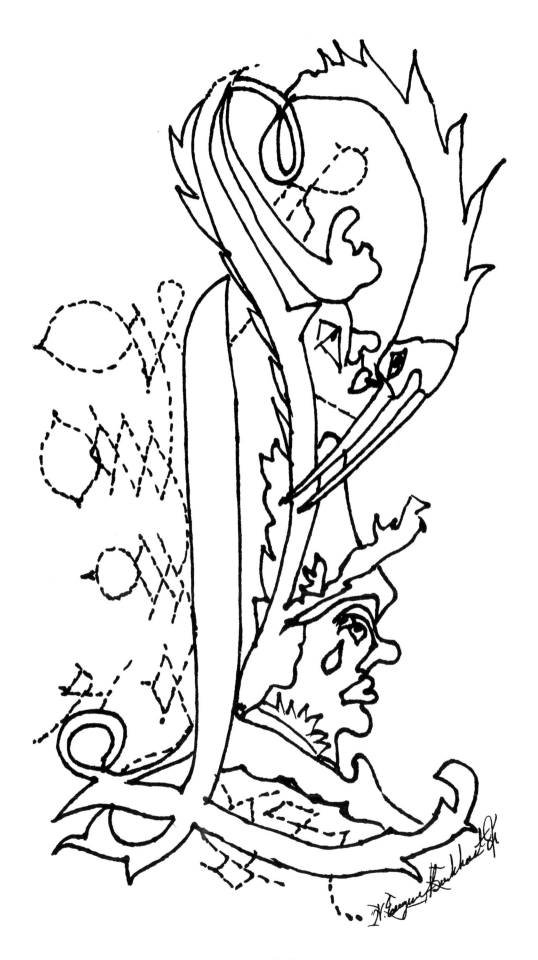

Plant List

River:	Hydrangea
Palm tree:	Tulip foliage, fern
Animals:	Cyclamen
People:	Cyclamen, poinsettia
Sailboats:	Cyclamen
Pyramids and mountains:	
	Various varieties of poinsettia

By looking at magazines, posters, photographs and art books, you will be able to find many ideas to create cutwork designs. Following is a gallery of cutwork designs with plant lists that I have created for you.

Leisure Garden

Plant List

Trees and shrubs:	Fig, parsley, China doll, nerve plant, fern, wild geranium
Clouds:	Pansy
Lattice:	Poinsettia, basil
Grapevines:	Maidenhair fern, salvia
Hammock:	Marigold, primrose, poinsettia, basil
Gardens:	Yellow sweet clover, verbena, delphinium, larkspur, heather, maidenhair fern, maple leaves, basil, forget-me-not, scaevola

Along the Trail

Plant List

Woodpecker:	Basil, carnation, cyclamen
Tree trunk:	Tulip foliage
Tree foliage:	China doll
Flowers:	Larkspur, larkspur foliage
Butterflies:	Marigold, basil
Clouds:	Pansy
Plants:	Lamium, fern, button fern, poinsettia

The Waltz

Plant List

Ceiling:	Gerbera daisy
Chandelier:	Marigold, carnation
Molding on ceiling and on walls:	
	Bear grass
Columns:	Bear grass, covered with cyclamen petals
Dresses:	Various varieties of viola or pansy, cosmos
Men:	Basil, cosmos, delphinium, pansy
Shoes:	Basil

Chinese New Year

Plant List

Dragon: Hydrangea, cosmos, delphinium, poinsettia, alstroemeria, dracaena, marigold

Wings of the dragon: Basil, nerve plant

Fireworks: Carnation, cosmos, delphinium, poinsettia, cyclamen, alyssum

Arch and buildings: Gerbera daisy, poinsettia, delphinium, nerve plant, nasturtium

Foliage: Basil

Clouds: Pansy, cyclamen

From Sea to Shining Sea

Plant List

Clouds:	Cyclamen	Flowering trees:	Alyssum
Ocean:	Delphinium, cyclamen	Trees:	Lamium, parsley, maidenhair fern
Sailboat:	Cyclamen	Steps:	Rose, maple leaves
Rock formation:	Poinsettia, pear leaves, maple leaves	Fence:	Rose
Pathway:	Maple leaves	Flowers along fence:	
Fence:	Rose		Caspia
Lighthouse:	Carnation, poinsettia, maple leaves, cyclamen		

Let Freedom Ring

Plant List

Background:	Carnation
Eagle:	Oak leaves, daisy, basil, marigold, poinsettia, primrose, pilea
Shield:	Carnation, gerbera daisy, cyclamen, delphinium

Courtyard Garden

Plant List

Sky:	Pansy
Wall:	Poinsettia
Trees:	Maidenhair fern, alyssum
Tree trunk:	Basil
Flowering vines:	Maidenhair fern, alyssum, Queen Anne's lace, statice
Fountain:	Poinsettia
Water:	Delphinium, salvia
Walkway:	Poinsettia, rose
Gardens:	Salvia, verbena, statice, Queen Anne's lace, bridal wreath, alyssum, lamium

Paradise under the Sea

Plant List

Fish:	Basil, pansy, gerbera daisy, alstroemeria, cyclamen
Plants:	Rue, fern, nerve plant, rabbit's foot fern, dusty miller
Coral:	Hibiscus

Bird of Paradise

Plant List

Parrot:	Pansy, gerbera daisy, carnation, basil, delphinium
Bird of paradise:	Cosmos, poinsettia foliage, delphinium
Foliage:	Salal, poinsettia
Bananas:	Gerbera daisy
Branch:	Croton

Grapevine Wreath

Plant List

Wreath:	Basil, lady's mantle
Flowers:	Cosmos, yellow sweet clover, buttercups
Foliage:	Astilbe, fern

SUPPLIES AND RESOURCES

A. C. Moore
www.acmoore.com

Michaels
www.michaels.com

Nature's Pressed Flowers, Inc.
P.O. Box 212
Orem, UT 84059-0212
800-850-2499
www.naturespressed.com

Temple Greenhouse
4821 Eighth Ave.
Temple, PA 19560
610-921-0791

International Pressed Flower Art Society
www.ipfas.org
Most of the activities of the society, founded in 1999, are in Japan, but the membership includes many pressed flower artists from around the world.

Pressed Flower Guild
www.pressedflowerguild.org.uk
Based in the United Kingdom, this is the oldest pressed flower organization, founded in 1983.

World Wide Pressed Flower Guild
www.wwpfg.org
This online international organization with members from all over the world was formed in 2001. Activities are online and accessible to members anytime and anywhere.

Pennsylvania Horticultural Society's Philadelphia Flower Show
www.theflowershow.com
This is the oldest flower show that annually features a pressed flower division. Initially the displays were beautiful whole flower designs and botanicals. In more recent years, there have been many entries with intricate cutwork as well as three-dimensional designs created from pressed plant material.